Cecil The Lion's Testament

A Novel

by

Bangambiki Habyarimana

Copyright © 2015 by Bangambiki Habyarimana

1st Edition

Disclaimer:

This is a work of fiction. Names, characters, businesses, places, events and incidents are either the products of the author's imagination or used in a fictitious manner. Any resemblance to actual persons, living or dead, or actual events is purely coincidental.

BIRTH AND EARLY YEARS

IT all began with a vision. It was in the last months of 2003 in the midst of Hwange National Park when Kat the Lioness got a vision at midnight. A huge light dazzled her eyes and in the light appeared an angel in the form of a lion that said:

"Blessed are you Kat, for God has chosen you to be great among lionesses. All generations of lions will consider you blessed."

Kat was terrified and cleaned her eyes with the back of her hand. She thought she was dreaming but checked herself and found she was awake, she even saw her sisters and her husband Muzi at her side asleep and snoring. She looked again in front of her and found the lion-shaped angel still standing there. Radiant in his glory.

"Who are you?" Kat asked

"I am Panthera Leo, the god of the animal kingdom"

"What does a god want with a poor lioness in the midst of nowhere at midnight?" She asked

"I am bringing you good news Kat. You have found favor in my face, and through you I'll bring about a new era of prosperity for lions and the whole animal kingdom. A golden era that will last forever. I have seen the suffering of lions, kings of the animal kingdom and their fellow animals. I have descended to give justice to all the beasts. From this moment you will never be the same. You are a goddess and all the animal kingdom will worship you. For you are pregnant and will bring forth two boys. The first to come forth will be a great warrior, but he will die in battle. The second one will be great among lions and other animals. He will be the messiah of all the animals. At that title, he will be respected by both men and animal. He will rule his lands with wisdom but he will not die a natural death for an arrow will pierce his heart. After that he will be turned into a god and all the world will worship him. He will begin the golden age of the animal kingdom and will be honored among men." Then the angel disappeared.

Kat the lioness was terrified. It was the first time he had seen and talked to a spirit. She had heard stories of spirits talking to people in her mother's many tales by the fireside, she had believed her and was amazed at the stories. But she thought those occurrences happened in the far past and were not possible today. But today a spirit had spoken to her. It was true: spirits talk with people even today.

She kept the angels words on her heart and thought about them every day.

The pregnancy grew day after day and she made plans to receive into the world her sons. She planned to put a mark to the first and a different mark to the second to differentiate them. And she prepared the signs. At the right time from the moment the angel said "You are pregnant" she gave birth to two boys and made sure she knew the first and second according to plan. But she immediately saw she did not need to put on them any signs because they were born with them. The first was born with no sign at all but the second was born with an aura like a rainbow that was always hovering above his head wherever he went. And she preferred the second to the first and would give to him more food than the eldest. It created jealousy among them and they would fight permanently. The oldest would always try to take out the rainbow aura that hovered above the head of his brother and put it on his own head instead. But it was impossible. Even when the youngest was asleep the rainbow aura remained above his head and would burn anyone who tried to harm the him.

The rest of the members of the pride were amazed by the supernatural crown that always hovered about Cecil's head. And they obeyed and respected him as they did her mother or his father.

Cecil also made many miracles. When a member of the family was hurt in hunt, he would touch his wounds and be healed.

His powers were known across the park and many an animal came to pay him homage and brought their patients to him to be touched and healed. Any animal who came with the intention to pay him homage and to seek cure would not be killed by the lions. But any animal that came with the intention to spy his lair or destroy his family was annihilated.

And it came to pass that a powerful medium and witchdoctor in a nearby village saw visions of a powerful young lion with a spiritual rainbow crown that made miracles and he came to make peace with him for he had received in a dream a revelation stating:

"Behold man and animal are brothers. From today they will live in peace and respect each other. For they are all my creation. Therefore I have appointed a Rainbow King who will rule over animals and humans. The human kings will consider him as their equal and respect him. Visit him and acknowledge him as your King. For from now on you have wo kings. The human king for your human side and the Rainbow King for your animal side. For besides being human you are also an animal. And when you kill animals you kill a part of yourselves and are incomplete. For it is your animal side that help you navigate the earth. Spilling an an animal's blood shows that a man is a heartless and godless creature. Unworthy of treading the earth. And as long as I am the Lord I will see to it that such a one will not enter my rest. Therefore call all your fellow leaders and your people, go to Cecil, the Rainbow Prince and pay your homage and allegiance as you do to your human leaders. By this act seal the eternal bond between man and animal."

And it came to pass that after hearing the revelation the famous medium who was respected across the country as prophet and seer by all, great and small, led a delegation to the king of the land and told him what he had heard from the vison. He told the king:

Your Majesty, three days ago I received a revelation from God thus saying "Behold man and animal are brothers. For today they will live in peace and respect each other. For they are all my creation. Therefore I have appointed a rainbow king who will rule over animals and humans. The human kings should consider him as their equal and respect him. Visit him and acknowledge him as your King. For from now on you have two kings. The human king for your human side and the Animal King for your animal side. For beside being human you are also animal. And when you kill animals you kill a part of yourselves and are incomplete. For it is your animal side that help you navigate the earth. Spilling an an animal's blood shows that a man is a heartless and godless creature. Unworthy of treading the earth. And as long as I am the Lord I will see to it that such a one will not enter my rest. Therefore call all your fellow leaders and your people, go to Cecil, the Rainbow Prince and pay your homage and allegiance as you do to your human leaders. By this act seal the eternal bond between man and animal."

The king, who always believed in everything he heard from the medium accepted and ordered all the leaders of the people to do what the medium had commanded so that there may be peace and prosperity across the land.

They were not afraid to go to meet the lions; for in a dream, the medium had received assurance saying "If you go in peace, you will be received in peace. You will not be harmed."

They went to the lion's den with a lot of sacrifices to Cecil the Rainbow prince and were received in peace. There was a great feast and speeches from the kings on two sides both acknowledging the usefulness of living in harmony with one another. Then the visitors returned home, happy that they had made peace with the animals.

Cecil the Rainbow Prince became famous across the country and many schools and hospitals were named after him. Streets, lakes, mountains and other landmarks in the country.

It was not before long that the name rang beyond the borders of the country and landed on television screens in publicity campaigns around the world.

"Come, visit the mythical land of Zimbabwe. Come, visit our mythical Cecil, the Rainbow king"

BLESSING AND SEPARATION

Now it came to pass that Cecil and his brother Leander grew up. They had reached the age of three and half years and according to lion tradition, they left home to find their own places.

Their mother Kat sent them away and blessed them saying:

"Go my sons, go and find your own places and live there. Be strong and fight well. You will meet many enemies for this is the jungle and only survives the most powerful. The law is eat or be eaten. Kill or be killed. I know many things about your lives but I know that you will be successful.

"Leander is the firstborn but will serve his younger brother

Leander is a mighty fighter and bodyguard to his brother

Leander is a great and feared prince

But the kingdom has been handed over to his brother

For Leander will precede Cecil to Exaltation

And prepare his Ascension to the Eternal Throne

Where Man and Animal will Reign forever."

Then she turned to Cecil and said

"Cecil will conquer his Enemies

He will establish a great empire

The Rainbow king will unite the lost kingdom

Of Man and Animal

He will be worshipped by men and animals

He is a god sent to the world

To right the wrongs

To straighten the crooked

Save animals from men

Men from animals

Animals from animals

And men from themselves

His mission will be completed at exaltation

Which he will not reach at old age

For a dentist will pull out his teeth

And by a bow will he be wounded

And by a bullet finished

It will not be the end

But the dawn of a new beginning

In man and animal co-existence

For the world will wake up

And roar in anger

Saying "Justice for Cecil"

For the slain Martyr

And the rights of animals

To inhabit the earth

Their original birthright

It will be a dark day for hunters

Whose sport is to kill

Wounding innocent creatures

Shedding natures blood

For pure sport

The hunters will be hunted

Beginning with the dentist

Who will be the most hated person in history

The Devils Brother

The Antichrist"

After finishing the blessings and prophecies to her sons, she sent them away.

She stood there and saw them as they disappeared behind the forest trees."

LIFE AND FAME

As nomads, I and my brother wondered around the forest, mountains, valleys and plains looking for the best place to establish ourselves.

We finally got in southern Hwange near the white man's pan where we made our home.

Meanwhile the campaign to discover Zimbabwe's wildlife especially it's wonderful lions was heating up and tourists and conservation workers poured in the country. It was by that time that me and my brother were discovered. We had by this time become famous because of the visit we had received when I was still young. We were being always watched and our movements controlled. It was not hard for the tourists and the conservation workers to find us.

We were very nervous to see men begin to enter our lives. And we regretted losing our privacy. They injected us with tranquilizers and put GPS collars on us to track our movements and behaviors. We tried to resist, but they did not use physical power which we know how to use, instead, the used technology which we know nothing about to control us.

They took pictures and filmed us and used the material to bring even more tourists to watch us. We were making a lot of money....for them.

Shortly after the encounter with tourists, we attacked king Mposu and his sons led by his older son Gen Judah ben Judah. It was a very long fight in which everything was used to defeat the enemy. In the end I lost my brother Leander, and Mposu was injured. I lost the battle and escaped alive and fled to south east of the park near Lukwashi. There I flourished and established a new pride of 22 lions. One of the most powerful kingdoms in Hwange. Our area was well supplied with buffaloes and impalas, so we had no problem finding food.

Tourists visited my kingdom and took photos. By now I was in all the albums of the richest people on earth: the Tourists. The ones who have the money to travel across the world to see wildlife and take photos and video of it. My photos and videos were posted on in every website and in social media. I was amazed at how people liked me and my pride. I graced the tourism magazines and was everywhere in tourism publicity. After the death of my brother Leander, I believed my mother's prophecy about me was true. I remembered the miracles I made while I was still young and the Rainbow I had while I was young. My mother had told me it was a sign to the animals and men that I was the Messiah. But he told me I had to live as a full lion and use my natural power to live and suffer what the animals suffer in the flesh to be able in a future life to be a Messiah who understood the real suffering of the animal and be capable to help them. I lived a simple life and patiently with both animals and men.

We had become familiar with humans and they would approach us in their cars. I wanted people to approximate their king and see him close

I would walk along with my family like soldiers and people were fond of our royal family.

In mid-2012 my kingdom was attacked by two male lions. Very huge and powerful princes. I fought valiantly but I was severely wounded but managed to escape with my life. I was expelled from my Lukwashi kingdom and wondered the forest looking for a safer place, I eventually reached the eastern part of the park where I encountered Jericho, one year younger than me. He was a nomad like me and hadn't yet established a pride. Our friendship grew each day that passed. And although we were not blood related, our friendship grew so much that we considered each other as brothers. We hunted together and fought together against our enemies. We eventually met a pride of three related lionesses and we courted them and became members and head of that pride. Being of a high stature and because of my princely upbringing, and my heavy long mane the women liked and mated with me.

From my union with Tara, the eldest among the lionesses came three cubs that are still young. I used to remain with them as their mother and her sisters, accompanied by Jericho went off to hunt. I would remain at home with the small ones to protect them against leopards and other attackers. In our culture the hunt is done mainly by women as they are more agile and unencumbered by the heavy mane we have.

I prayed to live some more to protect these kids, as the life of grown up lions is uncertain.

We are hunted down on all sides. We hunt each other for power and territory. Even if you are a powerful lion you can't hope to hold on to your area forever. There are always princes mightier than you. And life here is a constant fight to survive. There is no day you sit down and say "I have achieved my goal in life. I can sit and relax and live to my old age." That's not how it works here in the forest. We are also hunted by the ones who are supposed to protect us. We are objects, merchandise to be sold to the world. We are meat chickens. We are being grown here to be sold to the richest tourist to take us home as trophy. Instead of filling the forests live, men have created trophy houses for us, where we dwell dead, a type of sanitized hell. Hm, for a good lion is dead one, they say. It makes the state coffers full and the heart of the trophy owner swell with pride. Which king or wealthy man did not own a lion's head as a symbol of power. And what crime did we commit to embellish other people's palaces? When they put us in protected areas is so that they can sell us for the highest price not for protection. They don't want the common people to kill and sell us. But the common people are poor and they are not intimidated by law. They come in any time and kill us even in protected areas. When common people kill us illegally they called it poaching and when legally it's called legal hunt.

This is the world in which I brought my children. To live a short time, be hunted, killed and embellish a palace. Is it worth it? I am afraid these my children will die young. I have had the luck to live by this age. I have really survived. At thirteen years of age, I can call myself an ancient of days.

WOLTA PAHMA

Now, there was a man in a far off country who liked what they call big game hunting. His name was Wolta Pahma and he prided himself in hunting big animals like lions, elephants, giraffes, buffaloes etc. and was a member of an association of like-minded people who liked to kill for sport and leisure. He had killed more animals than he could count. His trophy house was a true cemetery but his appetite for spilling innocent blood was not satisfied.

Since the first time he saw Cecil the Lion on TV advertorials, his aim was to bring him back from the jungles of Zimbabwe to the right place where lions should live according to him. Cecil the Lion made a perfect trophy for him. For it was not an ordinary animal. It had a name, had a glorious family and history and myths were attached to it. He had heard the legend of how Cecil had come into being. He recalled that her mother Kat had had a vision of an angel one day during the night. And that the angel had prophesied a son will born to her that would be a god. The story thrilled him but of course took it as a legend, a way to enhance Cecil's power of attraction in the world. Nonetheless he found Cecil irresistible. He knew how larger than life he had become. But Wolta Pahma was ready for anything to own that unique trophy.

He went to visit Jack, a friend who liked the same hobby for advice and what to expect when wanting to hunt a lion in Africa

"It's very easy to hunt a lion in Africa. They only care about the money they get from the hunters. So we will end up killing all those lions and they will come to us in the following years to pay us to look at how a lion looked like. "

"What about hunting rules."

"The rules are in the books. Very well written with pompous language. But who the hell cares about rules when he wants to make months ends meet. Of course follow the rules. You could kill anything you want that's not on your permit. With your green notes you can buy anything and anyone."

"Do you know Cecil."

"Yes. Cecil the lion. It was named after Cecil Rhodes, the former owner of Rhodesia now Zimbabwe. The name was given by scientists studying it. It's a big, majestic lion with a heavy black mane. Everything you need in a lion. You can get close to it up to ten meters. It's very self-confident and allows people to approach it. Sometimes the pick up truck has to give way for Cecil want leave the track. I saw him and pictured him last summer when I went to Zimbabwe. Wait, let me bring the album."

He took the album from his book shelf and sat closer to him and they began to look at the wonderful photos of Cecil.

He made a virtual tour with him . "See here Cecil is socializing with another female lion, here Cecil sleeping on the carcass of a dead elephant while his pride is still eating, and here, the majestic Cecil accompanied by his soldiers, here....

"Magnificent. The true King of the Jungle. I'd like to have a look rather a kill". He grinned. Can I take that one? My trophy house doesn't have a worth king yet. "

My friend Pahma, you are really blood thirsty. So you can't look at any animal without killing it.

You're not the one to judge me; unfortunately we are both bloody thirsty bastards. Any novelty in your trophy room?

Of course, I brought a giraffe from Zimbabwe. Come have a look.

They entered his Jack's trophy room and looked at the different animals killed there.

"Of course this is beautiful, but no way near your world class museum. Cecil is too much of a risk for me to take. I don't want to be the proverbial hunter who turned hunted. Of course it's impossible to kill Cecil but you can make it possible if you have the guts. Cecil is the king of Huange. Beloved by the tourists the world over. It is a sort of celebrity. It's photos fill myriads of albums worldwide like this one we were holding in our hands and besides it's collared and it emits data every two hours. It's location is known around the clock. You need to be an FBI agent to whisk it away."Jack commented

"That's what I like. When it's really dangerous, it thrills me."

"Now then on your way. Talk to your guides in the *language they understand* and they will hand Cecil over to you. It will all go smoothly if it is done *professionally*. But should there be any leak, I guarantee its proportions will be nuclear!"

"Stop the doomsday prophecies and hand me the names of your "professionals. I am ready to risk everything to get to Cecil. If anything I'll go down in history as the man who got Cecil as trophy."

Jack took his phone from his jeans pocket and scribbled the names and numbers of some men who worked in Bush Safaris who had helped him kill the giraffe and had promised him assistance if he wanted anything. They had been his guides and friends while he was in Zimbabwe last summer.

Then he called one of the most known brokers there known as Bronx

Hi, it's Jack over here, yes, thanks. I have a customer here, he is landing in three days his name is Pahma, Wolta Pahma. Yes, he will call you when he arrives. Yes. His my brother. Ok. Take care of him. Thanks. Bye

After the call he handed Pahma the piece of paper. "I told him you'll be there in three days. His name is Bronx. An able man. When you get there call him You will be in secure hands."

Thanks pal. I am dead tired. See you.

It was midnight, and Pahma stumbled home. He was tired and badly in need of a sleep.

*****

Two days later Wolta Pahma boarded a plane to Africa. He looked through the window at the passing clouds. It was a clear day and the sun was shining above the plane. As the plane raced through the clouds he continued to intensely look at them as if he wanted them to reveal to him some wisdom. He was badly in need of it. He started to think about his life's pursuits, especially his obsessive hunting hobby. He thought "How many trophies do I already have in my trophy rooms. I feel like a little boy. They are my toys. I cherish them. The saying that men are always children and love their toys, except that the toys grow more expensive as they grow old is true.

Holding a lion's head in my hand makes me feel a man, not any man, but a powerful man, a worthy man, a warrior. In these days when men go to war and use automatic machine guns, or throw bombs to enemies from the distance, send out drones to do the scouting and then take out enemies remotely, I find no valor in those technologies.

In the end victory is not intensely felt, because you were so far from action or you had so superior weaponry that the victory was so easy. In ancient times fighting was real, not virtual, man to man. You fought with your own hands. You held your own sword and when you won you intensely felt it and gloried in it. You would shove your sword into the belly of your opponent and see his blood gushing out of his guts or you could cut off his head and see his blood rushing from his open veins, then you would really savor your victory.

I like bow hunting without firearms backup for this reason. I want to fill the fear of a possible defeat mounting in my stomach. That fear gives me boldness to attack a roaring lion, a terrible bear or furious buffalo. That's why I have to train seriously as a professional hunter. I don't want to rely on the superior quality of my bow only. I want to know how to use it. I want to be capable to run, make maneuvers, fight with my hands if necessary, a true master of the art of war. I want to merit the victory between me and the animal. I want a plain playing field where chances are equal. I don't want to fight a sick or helpless animal. There is no pleasure in fighting a weak opponent. There is no glory in an easy victory, that's why I want to fight a healthy adult animal, furious and ferocious ready to defend its life. I want a death ring. A gladiators ring against terrifying animals, so that when I win, I know that I am worthy of the trophy. That's why I love my trophy room, when I enter it, I feel a Caesar. I hope Cecil will rise to the challenge.

I opened my laptop and went to the album containing Cecil's photos and studied each one carefully. I wanted to be acquainted with him as much as possible. I studied his muscle structure, his claws, teeth, mane. I studied his possible weak points, everything I needed to know about him. But this was only a rehearsal. I had done this a couple of months ago when the project to kill Cecil had burgeoned in my head. Since that time I became obsessed with Cecil, and learnt much about him as I could. Know your opponent as yourself is an important axiom in our trade.

As I was absorbed in these photos, I went back mentally into his story. Of course, this lion had a story as I had. It was someone's son as I was, he had a mother and brothers, grandparents, great grandparents, a complete family tree from ancient lions to the beginning of the world. He had a history like mine, although completely in different kingdoms. He was from the kingdom of the hunted and I was from the kingdom of the hunters. He was from the kingdom of slaves I was from the kingdom of masters. He was from the kingdom of food I was from the kingdom of eaters. He was from the kingdom of brute beasts I was from the kingdom of intelligent men. When animals die, they cease to exist but when we die our souls live on. That's why we kill animals for food and for sport for there is no crime in that. We may even drive them to extinction, and we will find other sources of food and sport. So let me play around with them while they are still around.

My hunting carrier has reached its climax. It's the first time I'm looking forward to kill an animal so beloved by people. I am looking forward the titanic fight against this mammoth of a lion. I know many hunters want Cecil's head. But it's not for the fainthearted. These other so called hunters are no hunters at all. They are afraid of challenges. They want an easy kill and fill their trophy rooms with animal flesh and bones any one can gather anywhere from carcasses found in forests.

A trophy is something you fight for. It's something you want so badly. Something you sweat for. Something you are even ready to die for. Something like Cecil.

I am ready to do anything to get Cecil. Cecil or death. I'll pay whatever price asked. I'll even sell my soul to the devil to get Cecil. Cecil, Cecil is Mine. He held high the photo of Cecil in the air and cried loud: Cecil.

Everybody looked at him in amazement.

He said "Sorry."

One of them said. "Maybe it's the first time he is going to see African lions. He can't wait to see Cecil"

"Do you know Cecil?" He asked

Yes, sure, it's in Zimbabwe. The true king of the jungle."

"Oh my God. I hope I see him. I love lions." He muttered. His greed was multiplied tenfold.

He continued to think about Cecil until he fell asleep on his seat.

And dreamed hunting Cecil. He went through the forest with his three aids scanning the forest with their binoculars until they found Cecil. He pointed his arrow and fired and as soon as the arrow reached and pierced Cecil's heart, the ground beneath Wolta Pahma's feet opened and he was swallowed by the earth and descended to hell. He fell with all his body in the blazing flames and as his body was consumed he woke up screaming and all the people in the plane, terrified, turned their heads once again towards him, and he was once again ashamed of himself.

"Maybe he hasn't seen a live lion in his life. Might be having nightmares." One passenger who had told him he knew Cecil said.

He remained thoughtful through the rest of the trip and did not attach any significance to the nightmare he just had. He thought it as the first fruits of a combat to come, which he was confident to win, as always.

CECIL'S ADIEU

I was sitting under the tree after eating breakfast, and the children were playing in the grass in front of me and Tara was beside me and looked at me and her eyes wouldn't live me as I kept gazing in the void.

"What is the problem, "Tara asked me

"Thoughts of men, I am thinking about how I can be a better head of the family and protect you."

"Really? Tell me the truth Cecil. I know you are capable of that."

"You are right. I sense that our life is in danger."

"What do you see?"

"I see enemies everywhere; I see the hand of death approaching."

"But it has always been so for us. One more day of existence is luck for us."

"It has changed. We no longer have anywhere to hide. Neither the thickest forest nor the cave, nothing can hide us."

"How?"

"Look at that collar you are wearing."

"Beautiful."

"Don't be childish, Tara, since when have men been our friends. To lavish us with gifts?"

"Cecil, didn't you learn about Evolution, maybe they have changed to the best, instead of evolving away from us, maybe they are evolving towards us. Maybe they have found the intrinsic brotherhood between us. Don't you think so?"

"Skeptical. A responsible king is always skeptical. How many times have I used deceit to destroy my enemies. If an animal knows about deceit how much better man."

"Do you think these collars are a trap."

"Nothing but."

"I believe you. You are a great commander. Now we must plan how to respond."

"Too late, these collars control our movements. We have no more privacy. In the past we used to live independent in the jungle. We lived in our sovereign kingdoms, now there is nowhere to hide. The world has become too small. I see a greedy foolish man cutting my head and placing it in his trophy house."

"Why you."

"Greed. I am very famous. Look at the way they approach me, picture me, almost worship me. I am the perfect price. I see men lining up to cut my head to own the most famous lion on earth. I see the dentist's bow."

"What is that story of dentists?"

"My mother said so."

"Cecil, do you still believe in old women's tales? You are no longer a child."

"This no tale ,Tara. I have lived long enough to know my mother is no false prophet. No tale teller. My mother said my brother would die before me and it happened.

I was born on the word of an angel. My life is no ordinary life, and the god in me tells me it's time wind things up."

"You terrify me."

"Better terrified and prepared than caught unawares."

CECIL PASSES ON

Then it came to pass that the next day I sensed the odor of meat and followed it as usual. When I got to the spot I found a dead antelope and started to eat. As I was feasting on the fleshly killed antelope, I heard a whizzing sound coming in my direction and before I had time to find what it was two sharp arrows landed in my ribs. Excruciating pain ensued and I run away with all the power that was left in me. I ran with the intention to reach home as fast as I could but I was profusely bleeding and the loss of blood was weakening me. I slowed down and looked at the two arrows deep inside my body. I had nothing to do about them and the flow of blood continued non-stop. I pulled myself and hid myself beside a brush and waited for my slow, agonizing end. I remained in that condition for forty hours when finally my salvation came. The dentist had followed the trail of my blood, found me and sent me to my rest and exaltation with shots from his hunting rifle.

CECIL IN PARADISE

Immediately I saw myself leaving my body and ascending to heaven. I tried to re-enter my body but couldn't. I liked my body, my heavy black mane. I wanted to remain with my cubs and their mother Tara and protect them against incessant attacks. I loved the tourists, my friends, who loved me back. I liked how I posed for them to take beautiful pictures. I liked the awe they had when they saw me. I was sorry I was leaving them. With an indescribable pain I was separated from my body. I cried and wanted to return back.

When I was finally separated from my body I saw clearly everything. I saw everything before I was born, when I was born, all my life until death. I saw and knew everything.

After I was killed, the dentist lay his bow on my body and with his friends, all smiles, took photos with my body as a sign of victory and a proof they had killed the most beloved lion in Hwange National Park, Cecil the Lion. What a moment of pride it was for them. Taking photos with the corpse of a dead innocent animal who had done them no wrong, who never meant to harm them. For sport and pleasure, Wolta Pahma killed me. He didn't care when my blood was spilt and soaked the hot sand. Oh no, the blood of an animal is not red. It has no importance like the blood of a human being. For men are created in the image of God and they have an eternal soul they say. So in what image were the animals created? Didn't he create us too? Did he create us to be extinct or to fill the world and roam the forests, fill the air and the sea? It's a sin and a heinous crime to want to wipe out God's creation and anyone engaged in those inhumane acts will surely be punished either in their earthly lives or in the afterlife.

They then cut my head off my body and put it in a metal box. After that they skinned my body and lay it near my head in the same box which they labeled "MACHINE PARTS" in order to hide the contents and easily get away. They left the bare meat in the open for anyone with an appetite for lion flesh and drew off in pickup trucks leaving a huge cloud of dust behind.

Then it came to pass that I saw other park guards who were not involved in my killing, when they saw the illegal manner in which I was butchered immediately informed the authorities and the researchers who were following me and an unprecedented hunt for my killers was launched. The government announced that dead or alive the killer was to be found.

TARA, JERICHO AND THE CUBS

As I was dying and gasping my last, I saw my wife faint. Something like a sword went through her heart and she sat down and began to cry. My three little cubs approached her and consoled her.

"Mama, why are crying, they asked her in unison."

"I am not crying, she replied, shedding even more tears. I don't know my sons, but something terrible is happening right now."

"Where is Papa?"Kali, the oldest asked

"He went to hunt for us."

"Mama, is he safe?"

"I don't know."

"Will he come back?"

"He will never leave us alone. He will always bring something back for us."

"I am afraid also, "said Kitty the youngest

"Don't be afraid, your father is a great warrior prince and he'll surely come back."

She calmed the children, but she knew I was not of this world. For by the time I was killed, she saw my spirit leaving me.

My brother Jericho also felt it in his spirit. When he came back dragging the remains of an antelope with Tara's sisters he found Tara and the children sitting together in despair under the tree.

"Tara, I know what has happened. He said. I saw the Heavens open and Cecil sat at the right hand of God. But I will protect you and the children. Nothing evil will happen to you as long as I live. Cecil was my brother and our brotherhood will endure to the end of time."

Jericho approached the cubs and began to play with them.

My heart warmed up at the scene, and thanked Jericho from the bottom of my heart.

After seeing these things, behold, I was received in paradise by Panthera Leo, the great patriarch, the first Lion God created when he created the world.

He told me "Welcome to Paradise"

Then he ushered me to God who made me seat on a royal seat at his right hand and told me:

You are worthy of your Father. Seat and reign with me forever.

There was every type of animals in paradise and they all lived in harmony. Birds flew and sang happily in the sky. There were happy hippopotamuses, crocodiles, fish, whales and every creature that lives in water. They lived in clean, crystal clear rivers, lakes, seas and oceans in paradise. I saw impalas, giraffes, gazelles, antelopes, zebras, buffaloes, tigers, llamas and every ungulate we used to eat on earth living with lions and they were not afraid of lions for lions were not hungry and there was no eating in heaven. Everything was beautiful and perfect.

AFTERMATH

Minutes after Cecil was killed, the researchers failed to receive data from Cecil and were troubled. In their office the speculation was heated.

The man charged with Cecil and his pride in the department look was quizzy. He told his colleague:

"No signal from Cecil, can't find him."

"Not possible, we only changed the battery yesterday."

"This place where Cecil and his pride live is a dangerous place."

"Something wrong may have happened."

"We should always be prepared for the worst. How many time have we lost a cherished lion."

"You are jumping to conclusions."

"I am too experienced for that."

"Any clue."

"Of course. These days Cecil does not always reside in the protected area. Sometimes I see him wondering off to privately owned hunting concessions. And those places are full of hunters. If they had a chance on him, they wouldn't miss it."

"Maybe he is following some women there. There is a pride there with no men in it."

"Women, if he knew he wouldn't follow them there it's too dangerous."

"If a real man, of course he would follow women wherever they might be."

"Even in death."

"Of course. Women are priceless jewels and if you loved them you would follow them even into the pits of hell!"

"Wow, so romantic. But we're talking about a cherished lion, a pet of tourists, a pride of a nation. A lion we have the responsibility to protect. It can't be harmed."

"Enough. Let's make arrangements. Find the previous coordinates and we'll rush to the site and the nearby surroundings to see what's happening. It might be the battery, it might have been killed by other animals and the collar destroyed or may someone got hold of his head and destroyed the collar. Whatever the case we must get going."

While they were busying themselves to go down to the reserve, a panicked park guard erupted into their office without knocking at the door and stood there breathless and all looked at him alarmed, and before he had even uttered a word their hearts sunk, they knew it was bad news, terrible news. For his face was so grave as if a very fond relative had died. Thought it took only seconds to break his earthshattering announcement, these few seconds looked like an eternity to these conservation workers.

Then he burst out "Cecil has passed on."

Mouths went wide open, eyes filled to the brim, and tears slowly fell on cheeks. All three met in the midst of the room embraced each other, and silently cried.

It was a terrible day in their carrier. Cecil had become a member of their family. He was a brother.

****

Upon hearing about Cecil's death, the first measure of the government was to close down all the airports and all international land routes. Police were dispatched in all the terminals. And searches were conducted at the frontiers. Detectives in uniform and in plain clothes were dispatched across all the exit points from the country. But the search was handicapped by the lack of personal details of the hunter or hunters. By this time it was suspected it had been a wealthy Spaniard who had killed Cecil, and this theory was first advanced by men close to the killing of Cecil to muddy the waters and help the real killers to escape. So being a Spanish or holding a Spanish passport was almost a crime. And any Spaniard on the national territory was considered guilty until proven innocent. All luggages were suspected. All tourists were suspected. It was an undeclared martial law, and the detectives had almost plenipotentiary powers to hunt down and arrest the culprits.

Wolta Pahma had already taken his place in the plane which was ready to take off when the sound of the hostess from the loud speaker broke the relative calm prevailing in the plane. She announced: "Take-off rescheduled. Police to search plane. Illegal game hunt suspected on board. Please collaborate. As soon as search is over, we'll take off."

She had but finished speaking when four heavily armed detectives erupted inside the plane. Signs of panic were observed on passengers' faces who were terrified to see armed men in their midst minutes before take-off. They didn't like that. It looked like a terrorist hijack scene from the movies, others even believed it was a hijack.

Passports were checked. It all went smoothly and professionally. The early fears subsided as the passengers saw how the search was conducted. The detectives were rather calm and seemed to know what they were doing.

But Wolta Pahma was terrified. He was sitting on the far right last seat. As the detectives checked the passports towards him, he felt as if death's cold hand itself was coming to touch him. He thought the passport copy the detectives had was his. He sweated even though it was a cold morning. His heart raced. It almost broke through his chest but he managed to contain it. And told himself "Oh my God how the hell did I land myself in this trap." But as real fighter, his summoned his courage, and his adrenaline rose, he grew more confident. Dread of the enemy is your end. I must stand my ground. I must not be a coward. I can't die before the fight. I am the killer of Cecil the lion. I am a lion myself. I am proud I killed Cecil. I am ready for anything. This search is another trophy that I must win. And he regained his composure. He feigned to forget everything and looked through the windows and saw police going in and out of other planes. He looked into the air and the fog was clearing up and some blue sky was seen interspersed with some singing birds flying by. He felt a bit relieved. After all his documents were in order and he thought his kill was legal. As he was lost in his thoughts, a heavy hand landed on his shoulder and a frisson run through his body. He calmly issued his passport and waited in eternal agony for the sentence to fall but to his amazement, he was handed back his passport.

A current of fresh air filled his lungs.

Now one of the officers said "Anyone with a luggage bigger than 10 kg come near his luggage to be searched." A few passengers that had that amount came near their luggages.

Boxes, bags and other containers were opened in the hunt of the elusive Cecil until Wolta Pahma's "Machine Parts" Box. The detective asked Pahma to give the key to the box which he did reluctantly, as if he was handing over his own sword to be executed by it. The detective approached the highly suspected box, turned and confidently smiled to his colleague, kneeled down and inserted the key to the padlock, turned the key and unlocked. Wolta Pahma's heart was pounding so loud in his chest he thought other passengers were hearing it. But then something unexpected happened. Before he could open the box, the detective's phone rang and attended it while other officers were checking other luggages.

Allo, yes sir, yes sir, yes sir

After the call he threw the key to the owner and told his comrades. 'It's over. Let's go'

He had received a call from his superior that stated they were barking the wrong tree. He told them they were searching an American bound aircraft while they should be checking European bound aircrafts. He ordered with immediate effect to stop the search and exit the plane. He said they were losing precious time in the wrong places while the killers were escaping.

Order is order. You don't dispute an order.

The detective left wondering what was happening, why wasn't he allowed to finish the search? For the original order had been "Search every plane, big or small. No matter the destination." How the order came to change in mid-course was a mystery to him but he guessed what it meant when an order was unexpectedly changed. This was his country. And he had served so long to ignore the unwritten laws. Obedience was to be total. Disobedience was met with the harshest retribution. Forget about truth and integrity. Just follow the order. Truth and integrity in their profession were cardinal sins.

Wolta Pahma was awestricken, he stood there as a post, and as everybody was tidying up his affairs, he seemed out of this world, until a fellow touched his hand and told him: "Hey, close your box. It happened, it happens."

He came back to life, closed his box and went back to his seat.

And the plane took off.

****

As the search for Cecil's killers was gaining momentum, tourists updated their families about their holidays in Zimbabwe.

Rumors run like wildfires about what was happening.

Some fear-stricken tourists told their families that men in arms had hijacked their planes and were being identified to be killed.

Others said there was a coup in the country and all air and land transport were closed..

Yet others said all foreigners were held hostage and called for their governments to intervene.

Some more lucid people said it was an incident having to do with poaching. They told their families a rich Spaniard had killed a famous lion illegally and that police was hunting for the culprits. They assured the families they would be home soon once the issue was resolved.

All these rumors and half-truths were also spread online through the internet with headlines going like this:

"Rich Spaniard Kills Cecil the Lion"

"Hunt Goes on to Arrest Spanish Tourist Who Killed Cecil the Lion"

"Zimbabwe in Mourning as Landmark Lion Killed"

"The World Looses Cecil"

"The World Will Never Be the same without Cecil the King"

"Hung Cecil's Assassins"

****

Wolta Pahma's wife sat alone in the sitting room, read the scanty news. And she was full of apprehension. She knew that the man who had killed the lion was her husband. She had tried to talk him out of the pursuit but she had given in after her husband convinced her that it was possible to kill even Cecil.

"Lions have always been killed. We trophy hunters are respected people and are allowed to kill lions for we pay large sums of money for ou hobby.

The governments know the lion population is dwindling but they do nothing to cub the hunting. In fact they encourage us. Look at the publicity. Trophy hunter's paradise. Come get your prize. Come and get value for your money."

"But you know Cecil is no usual lion. I feel it could land us in hot waters." She retorted

"They will find another lion to replace him. Beside I am no petty bandit. I am going with full authorization. If anything happen I will deal with it legally. And my friend told me the other day that down there tourists are held in high esteem. He said a tourist is like a god and he can do anything he wants. He said with money you could buy everything. Not only Cecil but the whole national park if you wanted it."

Thus Wolta Pahma had convinced her wife and the next morning had kissed her goodbye at the airport and had flown away.

But her mood was now gloomy. She knew the reports were not true. She knows further investigations were being made and that soon the bomb would surely fall, and their obsessive appetite for animal trophies was going to shatter their lives. She sat their waiting for rigor mortis.

And it came.

Without knocking at the door, there appeared Wolta Pahma with his "Machine Parts" box.

There were no exchange of greetings. They looked each other in the eyes, and knew they had crossed the red line.

Then the unimaginable came.

The news anchor announced that the true killer of Cecil was identified as an American dentist Wolta Pahma.

They looked at the television screen with terror. They were the criminals of the day.

The anchor went into detail on how it had all happened. Gave the whole identity of Pahma, his profession and where he lived. He announced that the guides who had accompanied him had been arrested and would soon appear in a court.

Pahma's phone rang and he began to receive a deluge of death threats and hate messages.

Guards at his dental office called him to inform there were manifestations there and that an ad hoc memorial for Cecil was held there. They informed him he was hunted down dead or alive, that some people had put a price tag on his head.

He opened his website and his social media accounts and this is what he found there:

— "Lion-Killer"

— "Cecil-Killer"

— "Enemy of Life"

— Enemy of Humanity"

— The Devil,

— Dr Slaughter,

— Dr Trophyhunter,

— Owner of Satan's Dental Office,

— "Rot in Hell"

— "Pahma, there is a deep cavity waiting for you!"

— "Pahma, you are a murderer, you are a terrorist"

— "You're a disgrace to humanity and a detriment to our species as a whole."

— "Beware! This dentist might end up killing you in the process of whatever dental treatment you seek."

— "If you seek out a sociopath in a dentist - this is your guy."

— "If you visit this dentist for services, you are funding his sprees of killing innocent, magnificent African animals that should be protected."

— "Do not fund this sadistic man and his 'hobby.'"

— "I don't know about this person's capacity as a dentist. But in his capacity as a human being, he's failed."

— "Anyone who is a patient of Dr "Killer" Pahma is complicit and an accessory to murder of Cecil the Lion and the hundreds of other animals he has killed and/or poached illegally."

— "He had the Mufasa death scene from 'The Lion King' on a continuous loop in the waiting room."

— "I'm so glad I went to see Dr. Plmr. He did the most beautiful job on my teeth- which he personally carved out of elephant ivory."

— "Anyone who uses Pahma supports poaching and murdering protected animals."

He issued a statement "I am sorry that the exercise of the activity I love and practiced legally has caused this terrible incident. I didn't know that the lion I took was a local favorite and loved by many people. I am ready to cooperate with authorities on that matter."

While he skinned off Cecil's body and his head was hunging in his trophy room, he attempted to appease the revulsion and anger the world had against him. He tried to save his own skin. But will he ever be capable. He doubted. He remembered another dream he had early on the journey to the hunt, when he saw himself being skinned as he skinned Cecil and their fates forever joined.

He closed his phone and websites and went underground as he was being hunted down by justice and unknown individuals to answer for his crime.

****

The popular outcry helped crown Cecil the Lion king of men and animals. He was made spokesperson and patron saint of all animals.

Legislation in the name of Cecil to protect the big animals like lions, elephants, twigas, etc passed.

Air companies issued notices they would no longer carry animal trophies.

Cecil the Lion Church was founded where people come to pray with their pets. The motto on the door of the church being "Animals are our brothers". The congregation flourished and some members had visions of Cecil the Lion like church founder His Grace H. Cecil B

I was going home at night from work and an angel in the form of a lion appeared to me. He said "I am Cecil the Lion. King of animals and men. I have been pleased by your work for the animal welfare therefore I appoint you a prophet forever and knight you into the Order of Cecil the Lion. You are the first in this order, therefore go and order others you find worthy of the honor. Go my son and continue the good work you have begun."

We built a Hall of Fame for people and organizations who excelled in the protection of animals and a Hall of Shame for people who have killed animals for pleasure or have committed gross crimes against animals. Cecil the Lion promised they will never enter paradise.